CW00741454

Cello Meets Piano
II

Score and cello part

Compiled and edited by
Zusammengestellt und herausgegeben von
Compilé et edité par

Árpád Pejtsik

Könemann Music Budapest
K 239

INDEX

Sonata

G. Aldrovandini

attacca

Gavotta

Sonata

D. dalla Bella

Giga

Fine

Da Capo al Fine

Sonata
Op. 1, No. 5

G. Boni

Adagio e appoggiato

Allegro

Sonata

Allegro

20

Air
BWV 1068/II

J.S. Bach

22

L'arte del arco

Tema

Andante

G. Tartini

Var. I

Var. II

Var. III

p con espressione e tranquillamente

Var. IV

K 239

Var. VIII

Var. IX

f e largamente

con 8va

Sonatina

Hob. XI:101, 5, 108

J. Haydn

K 239

Allegro assai

Da Capo al Fine

Scherzando

Allegro ma non troppo

J.G. Albrechtsberger

K 239

Minore

Da Capo al Fine

40

Minuetto

L. Boccherini

Trio

Divertimento
from KV 487

W.A. Mozart

Menuetto

Fine

Trio

Menuetto da Capo

Rondo

Allegro

50

Andante con variazioni
WoO 44 b

L. van Beethoven

Var. II

Var. III

Var. IV

Var. V
Minore

Var. VI
Maggiore
Allegretto

Coda

Ave Maria
Op. 52, No. 6

F. Schubert

Lied ohne Worte
Op. 19, No. 4

F. Mendelssohn-Bartholdy

Schlummerlied
Op. 124, No. 16
Transcribed by G. Goltermann

R. Schumann

Étude-caprice
Op. 54, No. 4

G. Goltermann

Chanson triste

Op. 40, No. 2

P. Tchaïkovsky

K 239

Da Capo al ⊕
e poi la Coda

Coda

Appassionato
Op. 75, No. 3

A. Dvořák

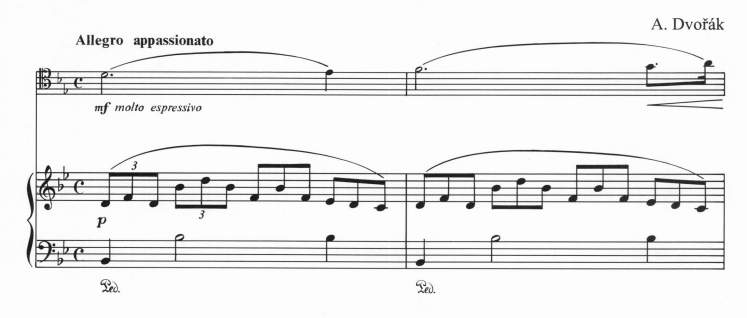

K 239

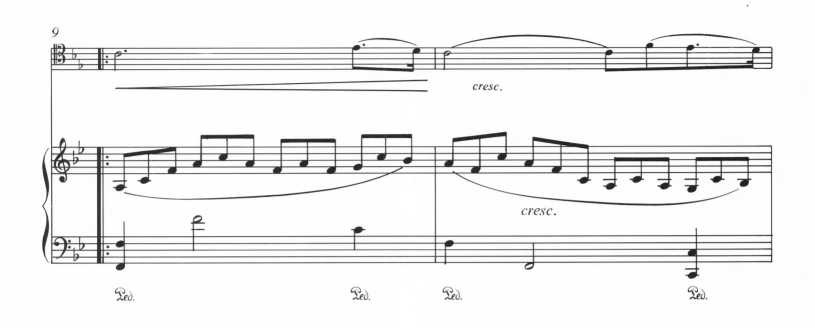

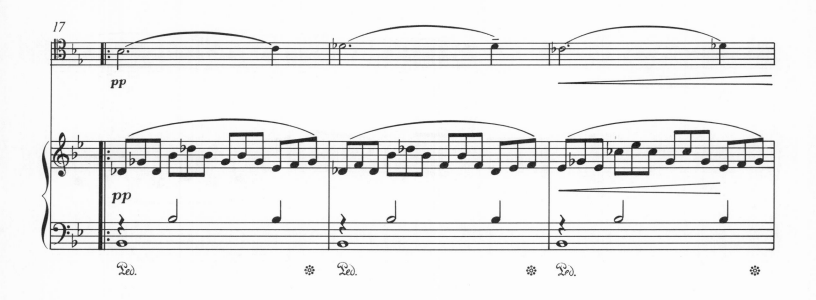

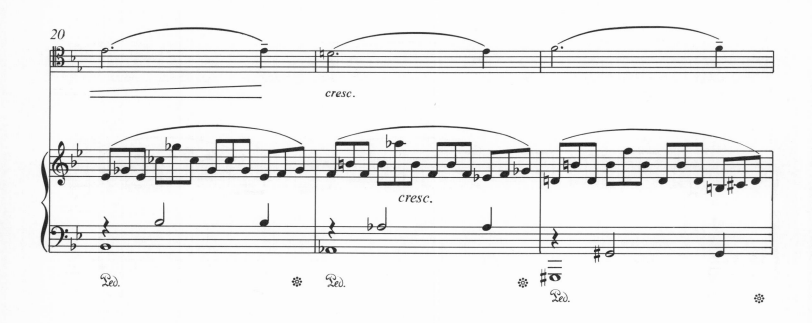

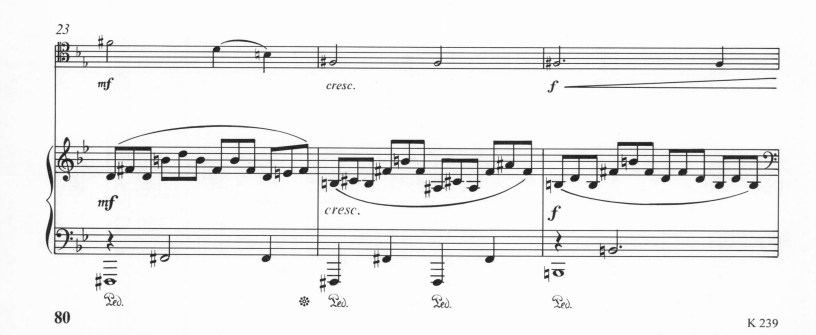

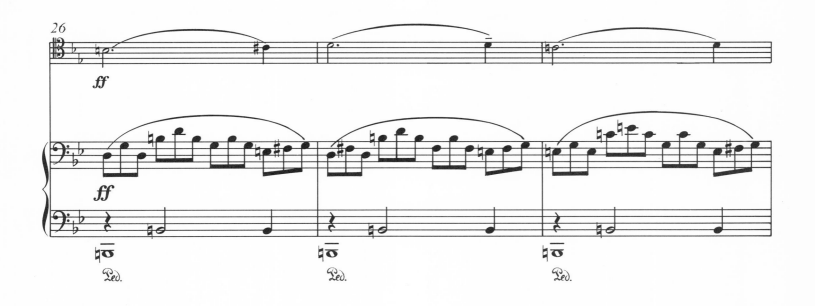

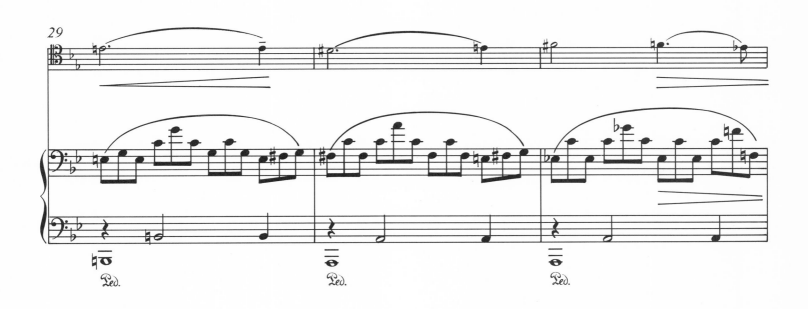

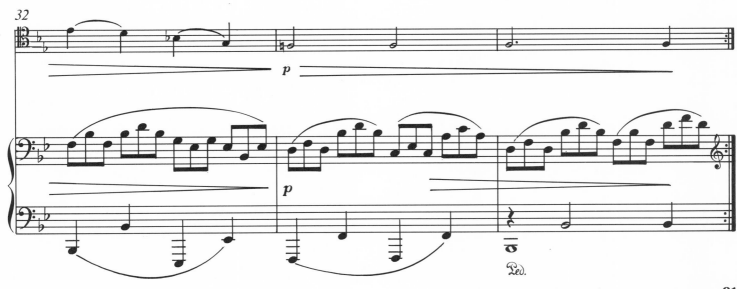

Air de Ballet
(Scène pittoresque)

J. Massenet

K 239

K 239

Poème érotique

Op. 43, No. 5

Transcribed by G. Goltermann

E. Grieg

Sérénade toscane
Op. 3, No. 2

G. Fauré

90

Chant triste
Op. 56, No. 3

A. Arensky

K 239

Romance

A. Skryabin

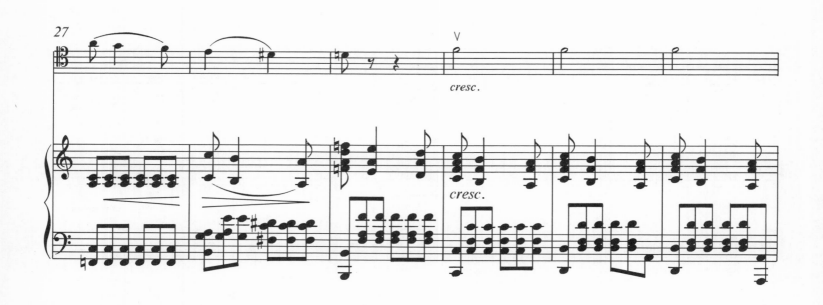

The realizations of the thorough bass are
by the editor of this volume. Arrangements are also by him;
exceptions are mentioned in the headings.

© 1997 for this edition by Könemann Music Budapest Kft.
H-1093 Budapest, Közraktár utca 10.

K 239

Distributed worldwide by
Könemann Verlagsgesellschaft mbH, Bonner Str. 126.
D-50968 Köln

Responsible co-editor: Árpád Pejtsik
Production: Detlev Schaper
Cover design: Peter Feierabend
Technical editor: Dezső Varga

Engraved by Kottamester Bt., Budapest:
Dénes Hárs, Éva Lipták, Endre Malaczkó

Printed by Kossuth Printing House Co., Budapest
Printed in Hungary

ISBN 963 9059 20 X